THE

AROMA

FACTOR

R

Relight House Publishers

Endorsements

'This book is written with deep emotion and reflection. I recommend it to anyone searching for inner peace and tranquility.'

—Mr. Joe Kerson
Head Teacher
RISE Education
Inspiring Young People to Achieve their Dreams

'We are pleased to read this thought-provoking testament. This book will inspire new thinking. We recommend it in a heartbeat.'

—Dr. Clement E. & Mrs. Juliana Otor
Public health BSC Honour. PhD and EMBA
Cambridge Technical adviser.
Associate Director, Leadership Management international (UK

'A thoughtful book for people who aspire to seek awareness and inner guidance; the passages flow through your thoughts and trigger emotions, raising questions you may have never asked yourself. I recommend it to those who are on a journey of clarity and self-awareness.' *—Cherie Johnson*

Cherie Johnson Family & Behaviour Therapist
Director of Shared Intense Support
BBI Young Entrepreneur of the year award winner 2015 Hon.
Southwark Civic Award winner 2017

'I just found another diamond—*The Aroma Factor*. A must have to help anyone to grow.

—*Henriette Djedou*
Founder of Diamond Ecoute

'This is a guide to facing the challenging but incredibly rewarding journey of living an authentic life. We learn that we can be the authors of our lives, and that we have the power to direct and influence our everyday life. This is a must-read for this modern day generation that is surrounded by a lot of distractions. People are increasingly getting more discontented, and the author brings our attention back to a simple life principle *'Treasure the Natural You.'*

—Coach Grace Oggudah
Founder,
Weather Proof Marriage & Women Let's Rock

THE

AROMA

FACTOR

Blending Your *Spices*

for a *Happier* You

VIDA LARTEY

R

Relight House Publishers

Quantity sales
Special discounts are available on quantity purchases by corporations, associations, and others. For details, contact the "Special Sales Department" at the address above.

The Aroma Factor/ Vida Lartey. —Sp ed.

ISBN: 978-1-9999195-4-2
Hardback Edition

ACKNOWLEDGEMENTS

I am most grateful to God for revealing to me my *Aroma Factor* and helping me to use it to bless my generation. To my loving and supporting family; my precious husband Daniel and our children, Thelma, Daniel Jnr. and Selassie for their patience and support during the writing of this book as a wife, mother, entrepreneur and a student, you make it easier to fulfill God's purpose and will for my life, you are awesome.

Having this book completed has taught me that we are the sum total of what we have learned from all who have taught us, both great and small. I am grateful especially to my angel mother Angelica Gle for nurturing me in love and wisdom; for showing me that I could become a great woman of essence and fulfill my purpose just like you.

To my late biological Parents Mr S.K Gle and Gladys Ackom you have helped me to understand the true meaning of forgiveness and love. You will always be remembered. So glad to have gone through the process. To my gifted Publisher, Richard Paa Kofi Botchwey for his diligence and keeping me on schedule, bravo!

My dear friends Dr. Clement E. & Mrs. Juliana Otor, you are an expression of pure love, you have been through the thick and thin with me, I am ever grateful.

Pastor David and Emilia Kwakye Saka your prayers and words of encouragement was my fuel. Mr. and Mrs. Eric and Rebecca Doku, I am highly indebted to you, Rebecca I remembered when you came over to cook for the kids when I was away. Henriette Djedou, you have not just been one of my best protégées, but turned out to be a great friend on the journey, see you at the top.

Mrs. Grace Oggudah you have been a mighty pillar, you helped me believe it was possible, your kind is rare. Thank you to all those who have encouraged and inspired me on this journey.

CONTENTS

AUTHOR'S NOTE

There is nothing more frustrating in life than not finding your aroma factor; the thing that makes you special, different, what makes you *you*. One person with the right aroma is greater than the passive force of ten thousand men who are merely interested in doing what their hands find to do. Your gifts will make way for you and enable you to fulfil your vision on earth.

Every person was created by God to be unique and different. God has placed in every human being a unique aroma and an assignment that is designed to give purpose and meaning to life. No person can give you your aroma; it is God-given. It is my prayer that you are transformed by the time you are done reading this book.

—Vida Lartey,

Chapter One

THE SPICES

Imagine a roast turkey without any spices. Not appetising, right? Believe it or not, every human being is made up of spices. They are what make us unique, what make us who we are. This is why we all have diverse fingerprints, looks, perceptions, and even DNAs.

Contemporary scientists are beginning to unearth the ultimate power of spices as weapons against illnesses such as cancer. "We're now starting to see a scientific basis for why people have been using spices medicinally for thousands of years," says Bharat Aggarwal, Ph.D., a professor at the University of Texas M.D. Anderson Cancer Centre in Houston and author of *Healing Spices* (Sterling, 2011).

For our lives to bloom in its fullness, for us to become fulfilled and happier at all times, we need to find our spices. Ginger for instance, can be used as a fresh root or as a dried powder; either way, ginger has anti-inflammatory benefits. It may help soothe an upset stomach as well as fight arthritis pain. This is also true about garlic and onions. In addition, dried spices like cloves, cinnamon, and black pepper all have high Oxygen Radical Absorbance Capacity scores, which indicate antioxidant potential.

Historically, there are numerous ways spices were applied; they were used in perfumes, aromatherapy, embalming, preserving and for numerous medicinal purposes.

Spices give life to bland foods; similarly we need certain key elements in life to spice us up! We can agree that nobody likes a dull life, but how do you ensure that your life does not turn out to be a dull one? You've got to discover your spices. And you will learn that it is in the discovery of our spices that we feel healed in our souls, ignited with joy and satisfied with who we are. Our spices drive peace and calmness into our lives and the lives of others around us.

When we discover our spices, we become the flavour of the world. Do you not believe that? Tell you what, when the spices from a Source Higher than yourself are in harmony with the spices of your physical being, the unimaginable happens.

There are five basic flavours common in spices which can be likened to the seasons of our lives. These are:

   i. Sweet flavour

   ii. Sour flavour

   iii. Bitter flavour

   iv. Salty flavour

   v. Umami (savoury) flavour

Life does not always taste the same. In fact, there are about five seasons in everyone's life. These seasons occur to grow us in different ways. When you understand that there is something to learn no matter which season in life you find yourself, you create an environment for good things to happen to you eventually, no matter what. The Bible says, there is a time and a season for everything. It is important to remain true to who you are and keep your spices intact irrespective of which one of these five seasons you may be experiencing at the moment:

A. Your Sweet Seasons

Sweet seasons are the most blissful moments in your life. From passing your exams to the day you say your vows, no one can deny the peace and warmth you feel when you are quilted in a blanket of comfort and joy.

B. Your Sour Seasons

Sour seasons represent a time of the ordinary. A continuous cycle of contentment.

C. Your Bitter Seasons

The taste of tragedy, hopelessness and pain linger on your tongue like lemon. It is in these bitter times that people give up and may even consider or commit suicide. A death of a loved one or loss of job can be counted as a bitter season.

D. Your Salty Seasons

You may experience jealousy, resentment and hatred from others towards you. It could also be a time of disappointments and criticism by colleagues or business partners. Your salty seasons are the times when it looks like the whole world is coming against you.

E. Your Umami (Savoury) Seasons

These are the moment where the light begins to shine again; new relationships forge, new job or business opportunities begin to trickle in.

Each season plays a key role in forming our individuality and uniqueness. It all depends on your understanding of the seasons and how you respond during these moments in your life. Embrace the journey; it will all work together for your good. And hey… take heart if you are in *the bitter season* right now, keep pushing and believing, your next season is at hand.

What Would You Have Done?

A certain King once placed a huge rock on the path leading to his palace one early morning. This was to find the wisest and most diligent amongst his kinsmen. From his room upstairs, he was watching to see who would take on the challenge.

Many of his wealthiest merchants came around and simply walked around it, complained and left despondently. Then came a penniless farmer. Upon seeing this huge rock, he laid down his wooden farm cart. After much toiling, he finally succeeded in removing the rock from the path.

Surprisingly, there was a purse beneath the huge rock. This purse contained many gold coins together with a note from the King. In his note, the King did not only gift the gold coins to whoever removed the rock from the street, he also invited the person to his palace. The diligent wise farmer was going to get knighted at the king's palace. In one day he earned gold coins worth millions of pounds. On this day, the farmer learned what we all have to learn; that every obstacle presents an opportunity to improve our circumstances. That, to be in charge of our dreams and goals in life, we must be prepared to take the rock out of our way, we must discover our spices and use it wisely for the good of society.

Chapter Two

HARMONY VS. BALANCE

All humans seek after one thing—*balance*. The truth, however, is that the spices of life do not work in balance, they work in harmony. It is considered a universal truth that every one of us desire 'balance' and *happiness*.

Many are chasing this *happiness* with the last drop of their blood. And yet, balance, in my opinion, is elusive and almost non-existing. Harmony, however, is attainable. The majority of us equate happiness to acquiring material things such as cars, great family, big houses, higher education, great health and so on; what we often call *'The Dream Life.'* This is where the frustrations set in, where many people let go of their dreams and just fade away like a cloud of dust. Michael Jackson had it all; the money, the supercars, the mansion, the fame, the talent, you name it, but sleep alluded him so much that he met his untimely death searching for sleep (rest and inner peace). He was overdosed by his own doctor. It was such a sad end of a *talent.*

We can only find *JOY* (happiness) if we connect with *The Master Spice Blender* (God). That is, if we put God first in everything that we do; we are able to find harmony and contentment in the midst of all the seasons. We may want to call it joy. *JOY* is an experience of inner peace at all times but happiness mainly depends on 'happenings'- the external things or what season we may find ourselves in.

The Apostle Paul said, "*I am not saying this because I am in need, for I have learned to be content whatever the circumstances. I know what it is to be in need, and I know what it is to have plenty. I have learned the secret of being content in any and every situation, whether well fed or hungry, whether living in plenty or in want. I can do all this through him who gives me strength."*

By contentment, I don't mean feeling comfortable where you are or giving up. This isn't about singing *'Que Sera Sera'* by Doris Day, to wit *"Whatever will be will be."* Nope! That's not true. Our lives are full of spices. Spices have great potentials and properties; we need to blend them together to flavour our world.

In a situation where life begins to feel bland and unfulfilled, you have to learn to (re)discover the source of your spices. Many people have substituted the name of the originator of all spices, GOD with *something else*. Some call it *energy, universe, the sun*, etc. I believe without any doubt that God is God. Period.

When the body, the mind, and the soul are in harmony with the Creator, you will truly be at peace. Are you struggling to find your spices, let alone blending them well for the happier you? I hope you are uncovering the secrets to free you from such struggles in this book.

The Spices– *the dilemmas of life*

I.   Who am I?

This question is about your identity. In psychology, identity is the qualities, beliefs, personality, looks, or expressions that make a person (self-identity) or group (particular social category or social group). A psychological identity relates to self-image (one's mental model of oneself), self-esteem, and individuality. You were created by God in His own image and likeness. You are not here by mistake. The creation story talks about when God created man, He put His own breath in man and immediately man became a living being.

II.   Where am I from?

We didn't just pop up here on planet earth. We came out of God. Genesis 1: 7, "So God created man in His own image…" Thus, it isn't about our earthly background; it's about the original source of humanity.

III.   Why am I here?

This is about your purpose on planet earth.   Dr. Myles Munroe said that "It is more important to know why you were born than to know the fact that you were born." You will easily begin to experiment with your life if you do not know why you exist. If you learn to make the Lord your source of joy and happiness, He will give you His desires. You can then know your purpose through your desires. "Take delight in the Lord, and he will give you the desires of your heart."

IV.   Where am I going?

You were not only born to work, pay bills, marry, procreate, eat, sleep, go shopping, go on pension and die; of course all these are part of our lives. We are here to fulfill an assignment. Your assignment is embedded within you. These are your spices. God placed us here to fulfill a destiny; to impact the future with our aroma. In helping us to do that we need to consider the quadrants of our lives:

THE QUADRANTS OF OUR LIVES

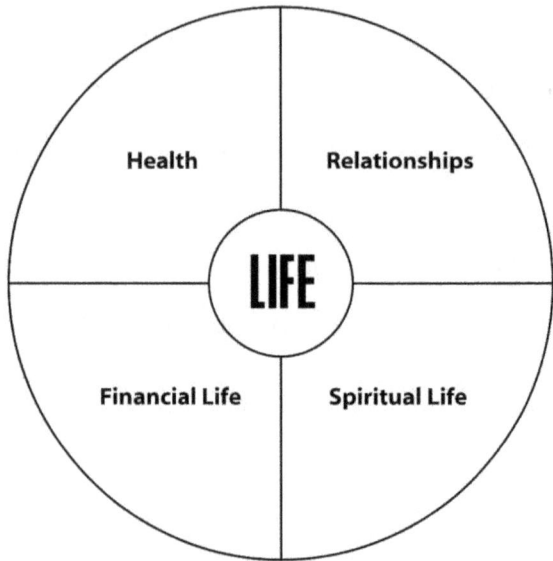

Health:

By this, I mean our total well-being– physical and psychological.

Relationships:

The family life: the way we relate to our spouses, children, parents and other extended family members. Our social life is very important too. The way we connect to our friends, colleagues, club members, those we share some common interest or hobbies with.

Financial Life:

Finances are of great significance to our existence. We work in order to gain income to meet our needs and the needs of those dear to us. We need money to buy a house, pay our rents, pay utility bills etc. Our financial life is propelled by personal development.

The Spiritual Life:

Our spirituality ties all the above together. This links to going back to our core because we are spiritual beings manifesting in the physical body. This is where we acquire wisdom, guidance, ideas, self-actualisation, understanding, and the power to carry on during all five seasons.

Would You Dare Embracing Your Spirituality to Hold it all together?

Following our own dreams and beliefs is often not easy. We're afraid of what our peers will think and how they'll react when they discover we believe differently from them. This is true not only of small things such as the colour of your clothing or the way you wear your hair, but also you wonder if they will approve of your choice of a mate or which church you attend. Does spirituality blend in with your lifestyle?

We want to be viewed as smart and intellectual and many times we're taught that intelligence and spirituality are two opposites that cannot possibly work together. Is this true? Surely, intelligence and spirituality can follow the same path and work together to achieve a common goal.

Spirituality is also the quality or state of being connected in an intimate relationship with God. Can we possess the courage to embrace our spirituality when as an intellectual person we find no logical reason to do so? Many of the enlightened and great thinkers of the world possess this courage to embrace both and teach that one complements the other.

The farther we pursue the paths of knowledge and faith, the more we learn that they support each other. Both knowledge and faith can exist well together; indeed, one without the other usually results in achievement without meaning and fulfillment. The perceived conflict between spirituality and intelligence does not exist if we follow each path far enough. We soon learn that the conflict is only imagined. What we attain in life has a direct correlation with our thoughts and attitudes. Positive thinking has shown that if we believe something, we can achieve it, but first we must believe in ourselves and our purpose.

There is no doubt we achieve more when we think positive thoughts rather than thoughts of defeat and fear. Thoughts of failure and fear sabotage us and these thoughts cause our own defeat. Expect the worst and you'll most likely get it.

God has a plan for success. He does not want us to fail and if we believe this then it makes intellectual sense to seek all the help we can. The Bible teaches that if God is for us, then who can be against us?

Prayer gives us courage to embrace our spirituality and to change ourselves, not God. If spirituality takes away your fears and allows you to move forward with faith and courage then it seems this is the smartest way to travel. *I am the vine; you are the branches. If you remain in me and I in you, you will bear much fruit; apart from me you can do nothing.* " God is the source of all spices. He alone can blend them well for a happier you.

Chapter Three

HMMM ....THE AROMA!

AROMA DEFINED

An aroma is *a distinctive, naturally pleasant smell. It can also mean a subtle, pervasive quality or atmosphere (presence).* Everything on planet earth has an aroma. And I mean living and non-living things. You can easily tell of the difference in those aromas even without physically setting your eyes on the object. If the whole world was to be in total darkness, and a Sokoto Gudali (a Nigerian type of goat) was to be passing, you will know. Why? Because goats have their peculiar aroma, or smell.

You do not need to be told of a coffee shop when you are in the vicinity of one. And this coffee aroma has won the heart of many in the Western world.

Do you know that God was inspired by the smell (aroma) of His own creations? Oh yes, He was. This influenced Him to create man in His own image so man can take care of His creations. You see then how special we are? As the scripture says, "God saw all that He had made, and it was very good."

An aroma is fluent in its own language; it speaks for itself.

Attracting Fake Aromas

Travelling is so important because whenever we travel we discover new and uncommon aromas that identify the natives of that nation. It tells us a lot about their culture and what kind of aroma appeals to them.

Aroma is what prolongs the existence of our worth. You can attract aroma from places you have been and items you have been in contact with. In your own home people can tell which part of the house you have been spending your time most of the day just by the aroma you carry. If you have been in the kitchen cooking all day everyone can tell, you do not need to say a word.

When you step out of your house, you may never return home with the same aroma depending on what or who you have been in contact with. If you have been drinking alcohol the aroma will give you out.

If you have been around colleagues who have been smoking cigarette don't tell me the aroma will not rub off on you. Be careful of the aroma you are attracting. That may not be the real you and many others could be tricked in to thinking that just because it smells on you it definitely belongs to you.

Many people today are trying everything to fit into a box that is not shaped for them, they are trying to be like everybody else, or what people are telling them they are; that is assuming a false aroma, it will not last, it will mess you up.

When you wash the kitchen clothes, you wash away the smell of food also, when you change those work clothes saturated by the smell of cigarette the smell fades away because you are not the person who smoked, you only happened to be around a smoker. Discover your own spices and make your own aroma and you will never have to keep attracting those rubbed off on you by the places you have been or the company you keep. Own your aroma. Psalm 1:1-6, *"Blessed is the one who does not walk in step with the wicked or stand in the way that sinners take or sit in the company of mockers, but whose delight is in the law of the Lord, and who meditates on His law day and night. That person is like a tree planted by streams of water, which yields its fruit in season and whose leaf does not wither—whatever they do prospers. Not so the wicked! They are like chaff that the wind blows away. Therefore the wicked will not stand in the judgment, nor sinners in the assembly of the righteous. For the Lord watches over the way of the righteous, but the way of the wicked leads to destruction."*

Attracting Genuine Aromas

In our everyday life we are surrounded by people. Some of them are a joy to be with; their loving and sweet presence helps bring the best out of us.

When we surround ourselves with positive people, we clear away the negativity that exists around us; we create more room to welcome the positive aroma. Their spices blend so well that it challenges us to blend our spices even better. Those are the people who believe in us; they push us toward our goals. Share your dreams and goals with only those who value them as much as you do.

"People are like dirt. They can either nourish you and help you grow as a person, or they can stunt your growth and make you wilt and die"- Plato

The Aroma of People

People are known by their powerful presence. Have you ever gotten intimidated by certain people's presence? Some people command such a strong presence (Aura) that when they come into contact with you, they may never need to say a word about who they are. This could either be positive or negative.

The ex-President Robert Mugabe of Zimbabwe was at the 72nd UN General Assembly. When he took his turn to address the assembly, the heads of states and all the representatives tore open the laughter that they had stockpiled. What was that? It was his aroma.

The world's greatest footballers, Lionel Messi, Cristiano Ronaldo, Neymar, and the rest, have distinctive aromas (skills), which have attracted many football managers and fetched them millions of fans around the world.

Whenever my husband comes back home from work, his aroma tells me that, he is home, even if I happen to be upstairs. Why is that? His aroma is speaking for him. When my children get back home from school, I surely can easily tell too. I believe you can identify with me concerning this kind of perception.

Our Aroma is what makes us distinctive. Ginger in any food is so distinctive, so are all other spices. They all have their properties and usefulness because of the aroma they possess.

To find your true essence of life, and to be a happier you, you have got to know what your true aroma is.

Chapter Four

WHY THE AROMA MATTERS

Your aroma factor speaks volumes about you. It is the impression and memories you live with people. It is really who you are and the substance you are made up of; it shows naturally even if you live a lie, but with time the aroma escapes and diffuses. It is your effectiveness on earth, composing of all four quadrants of your life. It is what people will remember you for, even when your life comes to an end.

The Aroma of the Master

The aroma of Jesus is a perfect example. What was it about Jesus that attracted people to him everywhere he went? Why was he in popular demand in his days to this day? The woman with the issue of blood, said to herself, if only I touched the hem of His garment, I will be made whole. His sweet distinctive aroma was speaking. She came behind Him and touched the hem of His garment. As soon as she did, "the fountain of her blood was dried up" and she "felt in her body that she was healed of that plague."

What presence do you carry? Maybe you have never taken the time to discover this important attribute about you. Pause; take a moment to reflect NOW.

Zacchaeus the Tax Collector – *Luke 19-1-10*

"Jesus entered Jericho and was passing through. A man was there by the name of Zacchaeus; he was a chief tax collector and was wealthy. He wanted to see who Jesus was, but because he was short he could not see over the crowd. So he ran ahead and climbed a sycamore-fig tree to see him, since Jesus was coming that way.

When Jesus reached the spot, he looked up and said to him, "Zacchaeus, come down immediately. I must stay at your house today." 6 So he came down at once and welcomed him gladly.

All the people saw this and began to mutter, "He has gone to be the guest of a sinner."

But Zacchaeus stood up and said to the Lord, "Look, Lord! Here and now I give half of my possessions to the poor, and if I have cheated anybody out of anything, I will pay back four times the amount."

Jesus said to him, "Today salvation has come to this house, because this man, too, is a son of Abraham. For the Son of Man came to seek and to save the lost."

Have you ever wondered what it was about Jesus that made Him impact and attract so many people to himself? Yet, many did not welcome Him. Jesus shows us that your aroma can also repel. If a person's aroma conflicts with yours they will try to stay away from you. The righteous and powerful aroma of Jesus was speaking for itself; it was overpowering evil and bringing healing, peace and comfort to those who got near to Him.

Yes, indeed, aroma matters. Have you notice how Christmas is widely celebrated all over the world both by

Christians and non-Christians? You can argue that Christmas has been heavily commercialised – that may be true but the atmosphere, the impact, the spirit, the joy and love on Christmas Day is so special and magical that it affects most people. The whole of England, for example, comes to a stand-still on Christmas Day. If you need public transport, *good luck*, you will have to leg it. What an aroma!

The Potential of Your Aroma

What kind of aroma do you leave on the minds of people? Who are you impacting and how are you impacting them? If you are a parent, what kind of aroma are you diffusing for your children? How do the people you meet at the school gate, the church, your workplace, on the train and other public places perceive you? Your aroma is everything; it is observed in your attitude, verbal and non-verbal communication and how you treat people.

The presence of some people just leave you empty, it drains your own aroma from you.

When you have envy, hatred, bitterness, spirit of competition, a quarrelsome heart or when you feed your mind on pornographic materials etc., you defuse negative or poisonous aroma.

I believe strongly in positive family values. It is the job of parents to pass on their aroma to their kids; therefore a parent's life should model after the adult they will like their children to become.

Have You Aligned Your Values With Your Goals?

Have you ever known people who would do anything to get what they want or to get to where they want to be? Maybe you've watched them be dishonest and take advantage of others to achieve their goals. They say anything and promise everything to get to the top and grab the brass ring. It may sound like we're talking about politicians and, unfortunately, this is true of many of them. But actually, these characteristics are evident in many of those we come in contact with every day in our businesses and personal lives.

It's unbelievable how many people are gullible enough to be drawn in to their web of deceit. These people sacrifice their values to reach their goals. It's said that if you want to be successful, if you want to lead, then align your values with your goals. If what's important to you in your daily living can help you reach your objectives then you're on your way to the top.

Values and goals must complement each other for you to be effective. But, if you struggle with anxiety and unhappiness as you strive for your aspirations then reaching them may not give you inner peace and happiness even if you're successful. Don't act like who you're not to become someone you won't like once you get there. If you don't like yourself, no one else will either. Define your goals. Of course, there are many types of goals and you must decide which is most important to you and your family. Most people when asked to define their goals first think of their career and monetary achievement. This may include material possessions and social standing in the community. These could coincide with personal and spiritual goals as you climb the mountain of life. Aspire to strike a harmony in all the qualities of life.

Define your values. What do you stand for? Is it courage, honesty, dedication, generosity, thoughtfulness, tolerance, loyalty? What drives you each day to get out of bed and do what you have to do? It could be love of family and God. It could be the thought of possessing power and money. Or, you could just feel peace in helping others achieve their goals.

If you're to be happy in your career and personal life you must align your values and goals.

A few years ago, when my daughter had reached infant school age, other mothers advised me to change my place of worship to a particular one that owns their infant school. They only admit children of active members. The idea sounded good and clever, the school was just a walking distance from my home. Also, they are noted to be one of the top performing schools in the borough. The idea was perfect but did it align with my morals and values? No. My husband said the idea sounded like sorcery; scheming our way to get what suits our ego is not part of our values.

I am happy I did not follow the masses, it all worked out so well, she later got admission into one of the top high schools in the borough. It is worth keeping our value no matter what!

You could fake it until you make it, but unless these are your true values it would be a hollow victory. Be true to yourself, work hard each day and you'll become the person you desire to be.

Who do you admire? It could be a famous person who exhibits the values you'd like. It could even be a person younger than you who exhibits the values you'd like to possess. There are many notable politicians, clergy, actors and athletes who live the quality of life you admire. The focus is not necessarily on their money but on their character. Aspire to be like them.

The person you admire and wish to imitate could also be a personal friend or a family member. Ask them what motivates their lives and how they aligned their values with their goals. If you're properly aligned with the values and goals of your life, you'll never regret where you are and where you will end. Aroma comes from realising your purpose. How you handle your aroma depends a lot on the decisions you make.

We were born looking like our parents but we will pass away looking like our decisions. The decisions you made yesterday is reflecting the result you are producing today. If your today is not bringing out any aroma, then, indeed, you made that choice in the past. Albert Einstein said, "Insanity is doing the same thing over and over again, and yet expecting a different result."

I always use reflections and prayers to examine my present situation, and if I feel my aroma is not working out well, in any of the quadrant of my life, I set new goals and follow them through. When I do, a few months down the line, I begin to experience the evidence of a *fresh Aroma*.

My Journey So Far

Growing up, I loved looking after people especially when they became unwell. I qualified as a professional Nurse in 1999, I was very excited and performed my duties with a lot of energy and enthusiasm.

I absolutely loved my job with all my heart. Often, I was admired by my patients and people I came into contact with. Their words of gratitude warmed my heart. Ten years along the line, that zealousness wasn't beaming any longer. Going to work became a struggle. Faking the smiles was the real deal – at least the job demanded it, and I gave it my best–you know *'the fake it till you make it' cliché.*

I put it down to working on the same unit for years. I decided to change jobs and I did. As the saying goes 'variety is the spice of life' but that did not cut it for me. I soon found out that variety by itself may not end up spicing your life; the spice of your life is better discovered in soul searching.

At one of my new jobs, there was a particular colleague who was a true manifestation of torment, a real poisonous aroma. The least said about her the better, she could simply not take my sweet aroma, I seem to be the sunshine around everyone and that made her feel insecure. Many of you might have experienced something similar. Remember some people may feel intimidated by your aroma; this reflects the salty season.

Questions flooded my mind nearly every minute. Deep questions jam-packed me. *Am I fulfilling my life's purpose? Is this job all worth the sacrifice? Am I going to be in this job till I retire? How would I be remembered when I expire?* I said to myself, no, no, a salary wasn't going to define my happiness. My destiny is not in the hands of my salary. There's more for me. Believe me it was one of my darkest moments. Maybe you are also asking yourself the same questions today, *take heart you will be fine.* You can smile at the storm; it is not as bad as it looks.

Eventually, I could no longer fake it anymore, no matter how much my heart was craving for that salary.

My body started giving me strong signals with minor health issues that couldn't be diagnosed by my Doctors. Everything I was feeling then was ascribed to stress. When you feel very tired after work continuously, check again, it could be you feeling uninspired. Dare to find your *aroma factor*.

I wasn't being the mother that I wanted to be, the wife that I'd always dreamt of. I hired nannies and au pairs, but no help can take the role of a mother and wife.

I am grateful for all the heartaches and the sleepless nights; it brought light to me. Today, I get the chance to speak at conferences, work with families, and hold strategy sessions with many clients facing similar dilemmas. This inspired me to write this book *The Aroma Factor*. I have travelled to many interesting places all over the world, still having the freedom to nurture my own family. I feel very grateful for the journey so far.

I believe the best is yet to come. I wish I had found someone to help me discover these secrets much sooner.

Nevertheless, I'm grateful. Don't let work related stress steal your aroma. Life is only one, so live it. Don't waste it, you deserve to enjoy life to the fullest. Take time to reflect on your life so far, and ask yourself if you are exactly where you want to be in all four quadrants of your life, if not, do not settle. Connect to your source; if need be, seek help from the right people: mentors, coaches, or people that have walked the path you want to take.

Chapter Five

MANIFESTING YOUR
TRUEST AROMA

Listening To Your Inner Voice

Y ou have an inner voice, and it is not a critical parent, an addictive personality or a compulsive spender within your head. It comes from the deepest part of who you are. It leads to real life expression. It does not shout; it actually speaks and communicates with you from a point of silence within you. Since it's a subtle voice, you need to be still and calm to be able to hear it. If your mind is filled with worry, extraneous thoughts, longing, resentment, stress, grief or fear, you will never hear this voice. It actually takes some practice to be able to listen to this voice. It is not easy to hear the desires of your heart. Sometimes, your passion will come as a serendipitous event or a whisper that will remind you of what is important and the things that can make you happy. This is quite the same to what's meant by trusting or listening to your inner voice. Learn to recognise your inner voice and you can do this by being in a state of calmness and quietness. You need to clear your thoughts with those unnecessary things that serve as barrier to listening to it.

One of the greatest secrets of staying in tune with your inner voice and understanding its messages is actually having a heart that is filled with love and gratitude. Open your heart, open it with great gratitude, and you will see that your inner voice will even become louder and clearer.

To create your life from your inner core means you are manifesting from the same source and intelligence as Aroma. This alignment enables you to manifest at the right time. When you sync your life with the soul inside you, everything is easier and more enjoyable. You don't have to try to figure out how to balance your individual needs with the needs of those around you.

In order to manifest your truest self, you must discover who you are. You must enter into a higher level of acceptance of your existing life situation and the actions that enticed it into being.

Acceptance is key as resistance keeps us entombed in the unwanted state. It is often said that "what we resist persists." It helps to send thoughts of love inward even as you ask your higher self for direction and comfort when the need arises.

Know that each step in your seasons of life serves you on your life's journey. Each step takes you closer to your truest self. It is therefore important to fully accept and trust in what is in your present reality to propel you through the process of becoming the ultimate you.

In manifesting your truest self, you should not try to judge or place any guilt or blame upon yourself or others. The power within you starts to diminish when you allow guilt, judgement or blame to seep in.

Instead, enter your place of inner wisdom. In there, you need to assess what may need to be forgiven. Also, find any wounds that need to be healed in order to regain your sense of harmony—the aroma factor. Once you regain your sense of harmony, the illusive need to continue any negative behaviour will disband. From this space of acceptance, trust, present awareness, and inner direction, positive and permanent changes will naturally flow.

Finding the Way Back To Your Core

Every morning, I start my day with writing my thoughts on paper, just to get them out there. It is a place where I can leave my concerns for now and believe that the answers will come to me.

Develop a Gratitude Mind-set

Life is full of uncertainties, and when things don't go your way, it becomes more difficult to focus on the positive side of life. However, if you want to improve your life, and ensure a positive future ahead of you, you need to change now. Keep your mind in a state of gratitude and constantly develop it.

When you're genuinely grateful for an event, a situation, a person or a thing, you are sending a great statement of faith to the source of your aroma. If you continue to develop a gratitude mindset and look at the brighter side of life, God will also bring positive changes in your life.

To develop a mindset of gratitude, you need to shift your focus from those things that you don't have to the things you have in abundance. Always be appreciative and thankful for even the smallest blessings you receive. Be grateful for life and for all the trials that occur to make you stronger. Learn to recognise the best things that are happening in your life rather than focusing on the otherwise.

When you develop a gratitude mindset, you will see positive changes in your life. You will also feel that no matter how hard life can be or how tough your problems are, you still live a happier life. Keep in mind that your happiness does not depend on others; it always depends on you. How you think about life today will manifest in the future.

Always be thankful for what you have, and focus on the great things life offers you. It is not always easy to trust that the answers will come or that the dreams will manifest but you need to keep at it.

To be honest, since I started with this practice, something big has shifted in my life. Practicing this principle truly work.

The Natural Connection & the Relief

A natural self-connection can be stimulated through all sorts of activities. A self-reflection time, keeping a daily gratitude journal, engaging in prayer sessions or calming breathing exercises.

Over time, my habit became 30 minutes of morning writing. I teach my children to do same; it is amazing reading their gratitude journals. Some read like; **'I am so thankful for the delicious chicken and special Jollof rice Mum cooked, oh mine, it was Yummy!!"**

Incorporate Gratitude into Your Daily Life

It is good to be thankful. Being thankful opens more doors. Your gratitude builds your mental strength. Grateful people feel healthy physically.

A 2011study published in *Health and Well-Being* found that grateful people sleep better (in terms of both duration and quality). A multitude of other research studies have linked gratitude to better coping skills.

My attitude has shifted and the weight on my shoulders doesn't feel that heavy anymore since I started keeping a gratitude journal. This is the natural way to express myself. It helps me to articulate and put my finger on thoughts, concerns and topics I didn't even realised were bugging me. It was in those moments of writing that I got the inspiration for some of the words I have poured into this book. Dedicating time to express gratitude has taught me to make time for myself, to connect with the inner me and to communicate in a different way with my loved ones. I am much calmer in handling things now and even the people around me feel the calm. There was a day my big sister phoned me to discuss some delicate family issues. She marvelled at my response, she couldn't believe how calmly I took the news. She said it took her days to gather the courage to call me because she knew my reaction to such issues in the past would have been very fiery. When you find your aroma factor everything about you changes for the better. My morning writing has also helped me to count my blessings and appreciate the things that already are in my life or have gradually appeared into my life.

Of course, there are still moments that I let go of my morning writing, moments that I just let myself be. But when I let things get in the way of my natural rhythm I get into trouble. And somehow the next day, I am even more drawn to my morning routine. I promise you'll testify to it as soon as you get into this habit too.

YOU WILL GET THERE

Learn to Appreciate What's Right with you now

We manifest so much good stuff already, but somehow we take it for granted. Those great seats in the theatre, the delicious taste of your own cooking, the company you keep at a wonderful dinner, or how you picked up that surprisingly good book, like the one you are reading now, hey…be grateful.

Don't forget that these are the aromas you've created around you. These are the moments to open your eyes for. These are the little aroma factors in your own day. I'm talking about all things that we as human beings constantly crave for, but when they are right in front of us, we don't seem to notice.

Treasure the Natural You

The natural you is there for support, for being creative, for being ready to play and make silly amounts of fun. These are your talents and they are there for you always.

Yes, acting in-sync with your heart and being truly authentic might seem scary at first. But trust me, relying on your gut feeling or spirit of discernment and allowing vulnerability into your life are things that will be rewarded in the end.

It is very much like when you try something new for the first time, you may feel butterflies in the stomach. But once you step up despite the fear, life suddenly grants you that boost of energy. And the more you persist, that scary 'new' thing becomes a part of your day-to-day life. I remember when I started *Facebook Live Videos*. Even though I appeared confident in front of the camera, deep within me, I had some butterflies in my stomach. Are they there now? No, they've all died off. The beginning is always the hardest, but when you take the first step, you will always be fine.

When you are presenting yourself in an authentic and natural way, your talents and creativity come out and you shine effortlessly.

When you are halfway there in expressing your authenticity– people start noticing that unique thing (your aroma) you are adding into your own life and into the lives of those around you –you will get to feel just how special you really are. Your aroma is your spokesperson.

If you're not sure yet how to manifest your natural self– ask around in your closest circle. What is it that your friend found interesting when he or she first met you? Also observe the moments you feel happy. How are people responding to you in these moments? This is how you will discover your natural talents. This great feeling will energise you so much that it will inspire you to be even bolder than never before!

Simple Steps for Diffusing Your Aroma

Everyone is already manifesting (may be not just enough.) The first step is realising how your thoughts, emotions, and visual imagery affect your life. Meditating on the word of God is connecting to your source naturally; it alters the flow of visualisation as well as the direction of your thoughts and emotions. It softens the negative emotions and opens the heart to love. This conscious visualisation activates faith, the salt and light needed to create a desire as the Bible says in Matthew 5: 13-16, *"You are the salt of the earth. But if the salt loses its saltiness, how can it be made salty again? It is no longer good for anything, except to be thrown out and trampled underfoot. You are the light of the world. A town built on a hill cannot be hidden. Neither do people light a lamp and put it under a bowl. Instead they put it on its stand, and it gives light to everyone in the house. In the same way, let your light shine before others, that they may see your good deeds and glorify your Father in heaven.*

You become more powerful when you consistently meditate on the word of God. When you don't consciously direct your faith, it takes the form of your lower thoughts, for instance fear. You also accumulate or store more faith, which makes it easier to navigate through life.

Your desires come from a higher source (God). He wants you to have prosperity, abundance, love, vitality, and a greater spiritual connection. Creating the positive in your life is part of stepping into your true identity. If you are consistently meditating on the living word, you learn how love is the magical substance that transforms your life.

I see many people today especially on social media looking very desperate; they post everything they do even issues that should remain personal. Some people post their divorce papers after a divorce and tell the story of their just ended marriage and how good it felt to be single again. Two months down the line same person posts about how to fall in love again. Desperation is a sign that you lack the aroma factor. Calm down and get hold of your truth, *GO WITHIN YOU TO GO ON.*

Creating what you want or desire often means "seeing" the opposite of your experience. For example, if you are unhappy in a particular area of life, you must see the exact opposite. If you experience financial loss, you see financial opportunities and possibilities coming to you again. If you are heartbroken, you visualise love coming from all directions in life. It's not enough to simply see it. You must feel and embrace it. You make the subjective experience more real than "life."

Lost objects reappear in strange places. Money manifests. You can grow younger, and opportunities appear from nowhere. The point is not asking how. Trust in the light and power of the all-knowing God. (You don't need to know how. Stay with practice and act when prompted from the inner self.)

If you share your desire with others, you are less likely to manifest it. It's best to keep quiet. If something brings spiritual and physical success, it's best not to discuss it outside your very inner circle. Spend your time helping others by seeing good things for them.

When you want to give up, you're probably close to manifesting your desire. There is a divine truth rule regarding manifestation. It takes a tremendous effort to manifest the last 5-10% of a desire. People often see success in the early phases, and they feel encouraged in the middle phase. They wonder if it will come into fruition in the last phase. It's very important to persevere through the last phase. It's the most difficult step. It requires a great deal of faith, but it is always worth it.

And you learn it's possible to endure through this phase, which typically seems to last forever!

After your desire manifests, you will feel happy and relieved. There is a temptation to put aside the spiritual work. You may be tempted to rest and revel in the results. (Don't give in.) Actually, it is the most important time to renew your spiritual practice because manifestation is ultimately about drawing closer to the source of your aroma factor. The closer you get to the source of your aroma, the more you realise that happiness, which comes from the inner self, is greater than any material achievement.

Chapter Six

PRESERVING
YOUR AROMA

L ike fruits and vegetables, your aroma can also decay. Hence the need for preservation. The fridge was made to help preserve food. Similarly, we must have a place to preserve our aroma. I will dig deep into that in the next chapter, where I will be talking about *Mastering Your Secret Place*, the store house for your aroma. Have you ever tried eating bland food before? Your aroma can taste bland if not properly preserved. When you are able to discover your aroma, you must guard it jealously like how an eagle guards its eggs. Research reveals that a female eagle puts in extra effort to protect her eggs. The male eagle assists the female to cover them with their feathers and nesting materials. Why do they do that? Because they know their worth; they know that they are special and rare. What we adore we preserve. Are people hungry for your aroma? Then you need to preserve it.

Most people may not necessarily like you but they are after your aroma. Have you realised that most famous people die off naturally the moment disaster strikes them and they lose their money or fame? People are after your aroma so watch out and note those who stick around in your low moments. Before we look at the ways and means to preserve our aroma, I would like us to look at:

Five Things That Can Easily contaminate Our Aroma

1. *Trying to please everyone*

We are in a world where everyone is looking for the approval of others. We post pictures on social media expecting our friends to like, we organise events and expect every single friend on our friends' list to attend, if they don't we feel unhappy and depressed. Put an end to that lifestyle. You wouldn't have been born if you were not approved. Stop chasing after the spotlight. You are the light, just find your spot and shine. *It is not about the mirror; it's about who you are mirroring.*

Have the courage to go your own way, to do it your own way. Always believe that your way will lead you to somewhere great. Don't tune in to the opinions of others when you have not considered yours. But if you think you are going to please everyone, you will be miserable. The ironic part of it is that the very people you are trying to please won't even appreciate the efforts. They are busy with their own lives. You miss out on living your own life when you spend time and energy chasing *LIKES and COMMENTS* on *SOCIAL MEDIA* or spending hours trying to prove your point to some random troll on the web.

Don't measure yourself against others. In reality, there is only one real person you are in competition with; that person is who you were yesterday. *'Comparing themselves with one another, they are not wise,'* says the Holy Bible.

2. *Living in the past*

Whatever happened in the past has happened. If you are fully present right now, then you can't relive yesterday or condemn yourself for what happened. What is gone is gone, it is over; it is finished. You can choose to live in the past or refuse to drown in shame and regret. You can let it continue to eat away at you and destroy your present life or you can yield to the fact that it already happened and make a choice to move on.

Trust God with your past. I believe that everything in my life is unfolding this way for a reason. I trust God and I believe He makes all things work together not only for my good, but for the good of others as well. Things happen on purpose, and when they do, my job isn't to figure out why; my job is to live and learn. If you cannot learn how to stop living in the past– if your thoughts aren't filling you with peace, joy, and power – then it is time to check what you think about. How? Write down how you feel about the situation. Tell God how sad, ashamed, and sorry you are. Accept His forgiveness, delight in His freedom, and immerse yourself in His joy. Then accept your past for what it is and live fully in this moment. You don't need to carry the burden anymore. It's not easy, but it is possible.

3. *Overthinking*

The mind loves to think, and it never seems to want to stop. In fact, we overthink so much that many people consider it a worldwide epidemic. It resembles a child who always wants to have everything a certain way and never knows how to have a quiet moment. If you allow your mind to endlessly run a mile a minute without ever interjecting, it will only press on with the madness until you discover that your mind has slowly become a prison. Learn to take time to keep your mind *silent*, instead of yielding to distraction around us. Allow yourself sometime for mental clarity, focus, and give up the toxic habit of overthinking.

According to Anthony Hopkins, "We are dying from *overthinking*. We are slowly killing ourselves by thinking about everything. Think. Think. Think. You can never trust the human mind anyway. It's a death trap." Psychology professor Susan Nolen-Hoeksema of the University of Michigan found that *overthinking* occurs mostly in young and middle aged adults, with 73% of 25-35 year-olds identifying as over-thinkers. Women (57%) and men (43%); we think too much, information over load kills your aroma.

4. *Rebellious Spirit*

There are times when we disobey authority and take to our own unruly ways. This is a very dangerous situation. It contaminates our aroma and it degrades us. Obedience is better than sacrifice. We must cultivate a humble spirit at all times.

5. *Being Prayer Less*

When we fail to communicate with our father we cut off the source of our aroma. Prayer is therefore very essential if we are to sustain our aroma. We will discuss prayer in-depth in subsequent chapters.

HOW THEN DO YOU PRESERVE YOUR AROMA?

Be Authentic

Every aroma has its authentic self. Be authentic like Jesus. Your words should line up with your actions. Your allegiance should be to God, who sees all things even in the uttermost secret place. Hold on to your values at all times. Be consistent in your relationship with God. In your low and high moments, choose to connect to your source. I always tell my children about the story of Joseph in the Bible, who was tempted by the wife of His master. Most young men if they were in the shoes of Joseph today would have taken advantage of the situation and even gone ahead to be boastful about it with their peers. But Joseph knew the glory of preserving his aroma. He did not want lust to alter his destiny (aroma). He took to his heels and I love what he said, "*I will not sin against my God.*" Note: he did not say *parents, master or even himself.* Married couples beware of this; if your affairs outside of marriage remain a secret, it does not mean you are being smart, it means your aroma remains a poison.

Always remember the one who gave you the aroma sees all things and you are answerable to only Him, *Not your wife, not your husband.* Be careful what you call a secret. Recently, some bigwigs in the political and the celebrity world lost their offices, fame and respect for things they did in secret many, many years ago. I believe some of the people might have even forgotten about those buried secrets but it eventually caught up with them. Your aroma will go stale if you do not keep true to yourself. Integrity is your way to a sweet and a lasting aroma. Never trade a short term gain for a long term pain. Apply this to every area of your life and your aroma will remain fresh.

Be Truthful To Yourself

Telling the truth about *yourself* to *yourself* is one of the fastest routes to preserving your authentic aroma. Before anyone would lie to you, they might have lied to themselves first. And in every lie there are two victims. The first is the person that told the lie and the second is the person that the lie was delivered to or the unsuspecting receiver of the lie. Although they are both at risk, the one whose case is worst is the liar. Honesty sets you free.

See Yourself in The Future

See yourself wherever you want to be. In other words, you must diffuse your aroma into the atmosphere of the future. While others are planning for today, check your diary for new projects in the near future. Some people expire on this earth because they are not sure of what they are here to do. The future is not far when you are telling the truth about *yourself* to *yourself*.

Traffic starts building up on the road only when you start lying to yourself, and eventually to the people around you. Hang around people who tell the truth, people who are truthful to their words. The truth is hard but once you get a taste of the freedom in truth, it's hard not to want more of that.

Move Out Once a While

Because of the weather conditions sometimes, you can easily imprison yourself. Inasmuch as *Home is Sweet*, nature is *sweeter* without any argument. It has amazing healing abilities. Every time I actually go to it for solace, it doesn't disappoint me. Many people may be frustrated in life because they have bought into the artificial world. No matter how expensive your house or car may be, you cannot compare it to the comfort that nature gives freely. Nature is so beautiful. You don't need to go far to get in touch with nature. Sometimes just step out of your house and breathe the fresh air for a minute. Take a walk in your neighbourhood; take a walk in the park, lean on a tree, or feel the wind on your face. Nature has a perfect aroma. I believe the seats in public places and the parks were built for us to take our rest. Nature is never lonely. Nature does not judge. Nature is a perfect friend. It is never a sin to move out to observe and appreciate God's creation. It rather makes God happy. So the road trips are good, going to the beach is okay, hiking is great. These help to refresh your aroma. Come to think of it, the air itself has a powerful aroma. Get out and get more of it.

Be Cautious of Aroma allergens

Aroma allergens are people or things that have the potential to destroy your best life, the happier you. You need to guide yourself against people who are allergens around your good aroma. When Judas was with Jesus he was not comfortable, especially when they were having supper together and Jesus said one of them would soon deny him. This was because of the negative thoughts he had in his mind, which reflected in his aroma. And yes, he denied Jesus.

Some people come into your life only to delay you; don't waste your precious time around such people. It did not go down well with some friends and relatives when I said I was going for my dreams. In fact, they were well meaning friends expressing their genuine concerns but it is good to believe strongly in your own aroma factor. Allergens are everywhere. They may criticise, degrade, derange and demoralise you, but stay focused. Never ever lose hope. Are you seeing yourself where you planned to be 5 years ago? Remember we are the sixth of the closest five people we move with.

Beware of Your Own Poisons

Our thoughts control our actions. We need to be careful of what we feed our minds on. Everything in the world begins and revolves around our thoughts. These thoughts mould and shape our aroma. Whatever you harbour in the innermost corridors of your thoughts, life will sooner or later reveal it in the outer arena. Grab hold of your spiritual truth. Like a seed hidden in a soil, it will eventually germinate. Our spiritual genes hold the creative power to frame our world to manufacture the aroma we choose to feed on.

During my publishing journey I met a young beautiful lady photographer called Helphie. After a studio session with her and some of her senior photographers, she was not sure her photos will turn out as good as that of the experienced professional colleague's. With all due respect to her seniors, when they delivered my edited photos, I was amazed at Helphie's shots— each one of them came out so well.   I now use her services. I will recommend her any day. She was under training then, yet you could smell her pleasing aroma. She is one of the best in the industry.

Uncovering Hidden Fears that are Holding Your *AROMA* Back

You might feel an urge within you to move forward, to do something to change your life, but fear is keeping you firmly stuck in your comfort zone. You want success, fulfilment and indeed your aroma factor. You crave it. But life seems so much easier if you avoid change rather than embrace it. It could be that you're subconsciously resisting change because of fears that are holding you back.

Not All Obstacles Are Obvious

There are always obstacles whenever you make a forward movement. Some of the obstacles are pretty easy to figure out. Others aren't, because they're not as obvious to us. Most people can recognise when fear strikes and they're afraid to do something. But other times, you come up with excuses, anything really, so that you don't have to face the facts and admit that it's actually fear that's holding you back.

There are common fears that are hidden in excuses that keep us stuck. One of the top ones is thinking that **you don't have time to reach for your dreams, life changes, success or whatever you are yearning for**.

This excuse is one that's used to keep you busy on the surface but it's a smokescreen for staying in your comfort place.

Everyone can find time to take a few small steps toward a dream regardless of how busy they are. It's just a matter of prioritising where you do spend your time. This excuse is often also feeling that you're so busy, that you just can't add one more thing to your plate.

"I don't know enough" is another excuse people use when fear is actually the driving force. Learning what you need isn't as hard as your fear can make you believe it is. It was a challenge for me to go back to university after 40, I took the challenge any way because the aroma factor has no limit to age, race, colour or looks. I am really glad I did; I am enjoying every moment of the wealth of knowledge available to me.

"I have time, but it's not the right time." If you wait for the right time, you'll never make a move. The right time is elusive and no one ever manages to find it. All you have is the time you're currently in. The best time to move forward is the time you have now.

"I need to focus on what brings in the money. I have to live." That's one of the top excuses people use, but it's actually fear talking. It means that they're afraid they won't have enough money to pay their bills if they make certain life changes.

"I'd really like to go for it, but my friends, family or spouse thinks it's a bad idea." This excuse is used to justify holding back out of fear of failure. If you can place the burden of not acting on someone else's shoulders, it helps you feel better about not chasing your dreams.

"The right doors haven't opened for me." Doors don't always open for your dreams. This excuse is one that's found in the fear that if you try you might discover there are no opportunities for you.

The thing about opportunities is that they don't always jump out at you when you're not taking action. You have to knock on the doors or you have to create the opportunity yourself.

"I don't know if I feel capable" is an excuse that hides the fear that everything won't work out. The truth is that not everything works out all of the time. If it did, this would be a perfect world. But if you're not moving forward toward your dreams, you will never know if yours could have worked out. Don't let fear of time, money, lack of experience, skills, lack of support, network or any other of the hundreds of excuses people use be the reason that your dream dies before it gets a chance to be realised.

Is Your Mindset Secretly at Odds with Your Level of Success?

You can have a fixed or a growth mindset and both can be used to bring you the success you deserve in life. Your mindset can be used to make your dreams come true. But your mindset can also be at odds with the success that you currently have. You might have a mindset that leans toward success, and you become aware that the success you have right now isn't where you want it to be and it's not as high as the level of success that you deserve. To get there, you need to take action steps. Otherwise, you won't break free of that mindset. You'll stay stuck. You can reach out to a strategist or a mentor to help you come up with an action plan.

A strategist can evaluate where you are and help you see obstacles and setbacks that may be keeping you from making progress. Some people may need to join a community of others who are also aiming to level up personally or professionally.

This can give you accountability, because they hold you accountable to goals you set. Plus, you get the support that can help you push forward. An example of this would be the group helping you find solutions through brainstorming, tutorials or advice. You can also have the kind of mindset where you're not okay with more responsibility being heaped on you. This can happen if you get a promotion at work or if you work for yourself. It can also happen in any area of your life, from relationships to weight loss, to financial desires. People who have a mindset where they're uncomfortable with levelling up and handling more responsibility may find it easier to avoid tasks that could move them forward.

Some people feel like they're not qualified. Your mindset might tell you that you don't have what it takes, but making action steps such as taking on more responsibility, will cause your confidence to grow.

You have to accept that the good things such as a better career or advancement, the position with the company, the dream come true or the rewards that come your way are meant for you. You deserve all the good things in life.

Patterns of Self Sabotage

Fear can cause self-sabotage. This can lead to you having actions, thoughts or emotions that interfere with what you want out of life. It could be a relationship change, a job, a move or anything you dream of accomplishing.

When you're experiencing fear, you might not even be aware that's what it is. But fear has a way of causing people to sabotage their own lives. Your fear might not be so outwardly noticeable where you pick up on it, but you can always tell when you're sabotaging your own success.

One of the ways that can easily become a pattern of this type of self-defeating behaviour is when you're pouring a lot of time into planning what you're going to do and what you want out of life. You're thinking about it, deciding how it all makes you feel, but you're not actually *doing* anything. This is spinning your wheels but never gaining any traction and without traction or taking steps forward, you will stay stuck.

This is procrastination that you may or may not recognise. When you engage in this, it gives you false proof that you're making progress when you're not. Another part of this pattern that's related to planning, thinking and feeling is perfectionism. You can become so busy giving too much time and attention to small things rather than focusing on what you want out of life. An example of this is someone who wants to start a business but they spend several months agonising over the font on a business card or the colour or the layout.

They tell themselves they're making progress because they're working on their dream when they're actually not.

This can be caused by fear so you drag out tasks that would move you forward toward your dream.

You have to face up to the fact that if you want something, there has to be regular forward movement. Otherwise, you're just treading in place. This can often be seen in poor time management as that's a way of self-sabotaging too.

People don't manage their time wisely so then they can say they can't do something because they're out of time. Fear can make you waste time doing things that don't matter on the journey toward where you want to be in life.

One pattern of self-sabotage is not having boundaries with yourself. You give in to things that you know will impede the growth of your success or the accomplishment of your dream.

For example, instead of spending time working on your business, you waste too much of it on social media. Or instead of levelling up your fitness when you want to lose weight, you choose to repeatedly give in to the friends who convince you that your life is fine as it is.

Boundaries, even for yourself, keep you from getting stuck in self-sabotage. Other patterns of self-sabotage can be not learning a new skill that you know you need to learn. You may just be only one skill away from your success or call it your real aroma factor swag.

You keep putting it off and then you don't move forward because you keep telling yourself you'll move forward once you learn what you need. Being too cautious while telling yourself you're just weighing the risks is another way people self-sabotage. There isn't anything in life that doesn't have some risk associated with it.

Practice Making the Leap without Struggling

Success is something that you deserve whether your emotions line up with that or not. Each time you have a success; it paves the way for even more success. This can often be beyond your wildest imagination. You can have more responsibilities, make more money or be faced with greater challenges than you had in your life before. It can be frightening to think about where you could end up, which is known as fear of success.

But many people don't realise that they're actually afraid of success. When you think about it, who wouldn't want to be successful? But people struggle with it because success can be unnerving, especially once you leave your comfort zone.

The key to finding your aroma without struggling with your actions, thoughts or emotions is to make sure that you increase the length of your commitment toward whatever it is that you're seeking out of life.

You might be someone who needs to feel comfortable with achieving a higher level of success and it's okay to feel that way. Many people need to come to terms with more success. The best way to do that is to gradually increase your involvement.

An example of this would be someone who wants to start his or her own business but he is afraid to leave the comfort and security of the monthly salary that he or she has.

You don't have to make the leap an all or nothing one. You can slowly increase the time and effort that you're putting into that business. Instead of giving up your job and jumping head first into a new business, you could start by giving the endeavour a couple of hours a day or a dedicated time every week.

You can make the leap gradually until you're more comfortable, as long as you're doing something to progress your new dream and you're not standing still. This applies to anything that you want in life.

For some people, that might be moving to a tropical island and working from their laptop. You can set things in motion that are geared toward you reaching your dream and then leap.

Eliminating Guilt to Enjoy Your Efforts

There is a downside that comes with success that you might not be aware of. When you achieve what it is that you set out to do, you might be surprised to realise that you're suddenly experiencing guilt.

Many successful people feel this way. One reason that people feel guilty is because they think they don't deserve to have what they have. They might think they were just lucky.

Guilt means that you did something wrong and far too many people who achieve success waste time, mental and emotional energy feeling guilty when they shouldn't.

You haven't done anything wrong when you achieve success. What you might be experiencing are feelings of wanting to be accepted for your success and for your efforts - but you can tell that not everyone is happy for you. Some people are struggling, while you're not. You're getting recognition and you're reaching your dreams while others are stuck. They're not able to get where you are.

You might even hear some snide comments when you've reached a certain level of success. While most people will genuinely be happy for you, not everyone will, and that's just part of life.

You can't focus on what others didn't achieve or what they don't have. Their journey in life is not the same as yours. It could simply be that success hasn't happened for them yet because they still have a few more steps to take. Or it could be that they had opportunities that they squandered and that's a lesson they have to learn. If you're feeling guilty because you're reaping good things in life, you need to realise that you're doing so as a result of all the effort and hard work that you put in. No one handed the success to you. You worked hard for it, and because of that you deserve all the good that comes your way. You aren't responsible for those who don't get to where you are.

The responsibility that you have is to yourself to live the good life; one that you choose to live. You are where you are because you fought the fear, you took the steps needed to make your dreams come true and you didn't give up even when things got hard. Indeed with the help of God.

Don't feel bad about where you are in life. You know the sacrifices that you had to make and those sacrifices and all that you went through to get where you are deserve to be honoured by the good things you now have.

Fears will rear their ugly heads from time to time. Sometimes it will be very obvious to you and other times you'll refuse to acknowledge that what you have labelled as a real concern is nothing more than baseless anxiety of what may or may not happen as a result of your efforts.

The good news is, the more you open your eyes to what holds you back, the more aware you are for future obstacles, and you'll be able to move past it quickly and recover your progress easily. Whatever it takes, you need your aroma factor!

Chapter Seven

MASTERING YOUR SECRET PLACE

He who dwells in the *Secret Place* of the Most High shall abide under the shadow of the Almighty." Matthew and Rose were a newly wedded couple who invited me for dinner one night in spring at their home. I sat and listened to them as they uncover deep issues about how unhappy they felt living as a couple. I allowed them to express all their concerns about each other. The main issue I picked up was that they both relied on each other for their happiness. They had only been married for a little less than a year. I could easily tell they never really discovered themselves before coming together. I had to take them through a deep self-discovery programme for six weeks. By the end of the programme, they were totally transformed than I had met them. They now understand that we are all responsible for our own happiness; no one can ever make us happy. Going back to your source for his unchanging love each day and relying on His power to walk through the valleys of life is very key. The power of heaven is unlocked on earth when we dedicate ourselves to the secret place of the Most High.

The strength of your aroma lies in Your Closeness to The Most High God. Think carefully about your inner chamber; will you allow strangers in there? No– It's your *Secret Place*. Many people are running helter-skelter, barging into churches, calling all kinds of spirits to help sharpen their aroma. Others go for counselling sessions for many years, but you have to understand that all these specialists can only give you guidelines, here again it will take your own determination and effort. No one else can take care of your relationship with your father except yourself. We need to build that secret altar ourselves, learning to draw strength from His sweet presence always. Are you going to stay in your secret place as Jesus did? I imagine that every morning the Saviour went to His secret place to meet with His father. He therefore only said a word to the sick or any obstacle and then miracles followed Him. Note: *He did not follow miracles.*

God wants to reveal Himself to us. But His most cherished creation is not in constant touch with Him. We have not always kept our part of the deal. We must check on Him every morning. He needs us to stay closest to Him, to show our gratitude for the small things and even for the gift of life. He alone can reveal our assignment to us. Stop chasing the blessing and chase after the source of all things. Put Him first, in all things, He is the source of our aroma factor.

WHAT THE SECRET PLACE IS NOT

The secret place is not your church (or any building) It is not your pastor or holy oil or water. It is not an image or any physical object.

Looking at the competition among churches today and the fashion we have adopted in the church it makes me wonder if God dwells in our earthly buildings.

✳ The Secret Place is Not Your Marriage

✳ The Secret Place is Not Your Children

✳ The Secret Place is Not Your House

✳ The Secret Place is not Your Degree

When you were born, you signed an agreement automatically that you will stay in touch with God. But because we are human beings, our minds change constantly. The amazing thing about God is that He is still the God of yesterday, today and forever. God is ready to accept us. It is time to enter into your secret place.

BENEFITS OF THE SECRET PLACE

The secret place is refreshing

The secret place is inspiring

The secret place gives you brilliant ideas

The secret place is your hiding place

The secret place brings healing

The secret place gives you the aroma factor

If you want to have the aroma of Jesus, then you must keep close to your secret place every day. Tie yourself to your secret place to seek your Father (God). The fastest ferry to finding and pursuing greatness is in your constant touch with the source of your aroma.

Chapter Eight

THE PRICE TAG
OF YOUR AROMA

When Apple Inc. released the first iPhone in 2007, I was one of their buyers. Owning one was a big deal. A few months later, Apple announced that they were releasing a new model; iPhone 4. The price of the first model dropped instantly. As you know, the newest models are always the most expensive ones until a newer version is released. This applies to a lot of commodities. Just before Christmas in the UK, lots of shops were fully stocked up with new Christmas arrivals selling at full prices. On Boxing Day these same commodities are reduced drastically, some more than 50%, now the question is why is it so? The quality remains the same but indeed the entrepreneur needs to make room for new items arriving. As humans, if we are not mindful of who we are, with time, we also begin to act like commodities on the shop shelves, but we are not. The aroma factor you had with you from the day you were born will never change. A lot of young ladies have lost some great young suitors because of the trend and vice versa. I remember a mate of mine rejected a young man, who had only started his very first job after graduation from university. He had no car, no fancy clothes and was paid a low salary. He later became the CEO of his own company. My mate is on her third miserable marriage. What a tragedy.

Trends Don't Last

Trends begin to pass away when people no longer see them as new and exceptional. We are all getting lost by chasing the newest commodity on the market to boost our self-worth or self-esteem— the aroma factor.

We live in a world where the pace keeps getting faster. We are blasted by information and ideas we cannot digest. We are all almost lost in the noise. The trends can destroy marriages and lead to financial constraints and a lack of solid financial plans for the future. Certain couples want to always be the best dressed at every function but they actually have no love and peace beyond their outfits. It is worth noting that children pick up financial and spending habits from parents so this foolishness must stop.

Are You Damaging Your Child's Price Tag (Self-Esteem)?

Self-esteem is important for any child's development. They need it to grow into a confident adult later in life. When a child has low self-esteem, he has a tougher time handling his everyday troubles. Further, he might grow up with the same level of self-esteem, creating an adult who cannot take charge of his own life.

In severe cases, children have resorted to committing suicide over low self-esteem issues.

In order for them to start building confidence and believe in themselves, you'll need to sit back and take a look at what you're doing to encourage them in their lives. Your child needs your guidance and nurturing all throughout his life. Some of the mistakes that parents make with their children, without even realising it, are focusing too much on their children's weaknesses and not enough on their strengths.

No child, or adult for that matter, is perfect so there's no need to constantly remind them of that every day. Children need to be taught right from wrong, but you shouldn't harp on the fact that they never get anything right.

You're there to help them realise their mistakes, help them to learn from them, and show them how to change paths and turn something from a negative into a positive. Focusing on the mistakes they make will only lower their self-esteem and make them feel like they can't do anything right. Some children only hear the negative things and nothing about the positive. At times parents forget to praise their children for the good things they do. It's those moments of praise in a child's life that allows them to build confidence within themselves.

Every so often children need to be given a little more responsibility so that they have ample opportunity to achieve something. Those who aren't given the chance equate it with not being good enough to do anything. It dampers their spirit and will eventually control them to the point where they won't *want* to try to achieve anything for fear of failure. Give them some kind of responsibility that's appropriate for their age and skillset.

Children look up to their parents. In their eyes, you're superhuman, but that can result in low confidence in themselves when they start to think that they could never live up to you.

Don't be afraid to let them know (and see) your imperfections. It's a lot easier on them when they realise that you make mistakes too. For families with more than one child, competition arises for their parent's attention and affection.

Each child needs to be treated individually according to their needs, but the accolades they receive should be equal in abundance. Help your child deal with the turmoil of everyday life as they move from childhood to adulthood by building their self-esteem a little bit each day.

You Are Not a Commodity

You are not a commodity. There is no new model after you. You are the original one. Never change your price tag.

When a Bad Relationship Damages Your Self-Esteem

Getting involved in a bad relationship is something that a lot of people go through at one time or another. Sometimes, people endure mental abuse from their partners, and this can have a lasting negative effect on them. It can be tough to bounce back from mental abuse and your self-esteem suffers greatly because of it. Mental abuse is usually an attack by your partner to make you feel worthless and insecure. The partner does this to gain control and boost his or her own ego (yes, women too can be abusive). They want you to have low self-esteem so you won't think for yourself. Getting out of a relationship like that is the first step you need to take in order to save your own sanity.

There are other things you'll need to do to bounce back from mental abuse. It's important to stay active. Get out and do things with your family and friends, because an abuser loves to alienate you from your loved ones. Keep your mind focused on other things so that you don't isolate yourself at home and become dependent on the negative person who's feeding into your self-esteem issues. Pray, call up friends, read uplifting books or concentrate on a project like redecorating your house.

Do whatever it takes to keep you going. If you have a job, continue to work and take note of your goals and achievements. If you don't have a job, look for one. Working can get your mind off your problems and give you the necessary affirmation that you can do whatever you put your mind to - and that you're not worthless.

Avoid jumping into other relationships until you're fully healed emotionally. You're more likely to fall for other partners who are just like your ex. You don't want to get into the same situation as before and repeat the cycle of abuse.

Don't waste time thinking about your ex; whether it's negative or otherwise. Some people make the mistake of spending a lot of time with thoughts of how much they hate their former partner or how they wish they could get revenge. Release the anger and focus on what's important– you! It's time to move forward with your life. Don't be afraid to seek some professional help. A professional can help you work through your feelings and help you build your self-esteem back up. Don't let a bad relationship break your spirit.

We are 'storehouses' occupied with choice 'items,' which I talked about in the previous chapters. And all these items come with a price tag. There is a price tag to your aroma. Do not allow anyone, anything, or any tragedy to change your price tag. You are a precious gem, no matter where you find yourself or what happens to you, your value remains the same, with the passage of time, your value may even increase. That is the real aroma factor.

Become an Optimist to Experience Less Stress

It's a scientifically proven fact that those who see the world in a "glass half full" kind of way live longer and experience less stress. Doctors claim that a big majority of all of their office calls are for chronic stress-related health woes, so it makes sense that if you see the world with a positive mindset, you'd have fewer physical and mental problems.

When researchers at Concordia University conducted a study about pessimists and optimists, they discovered a direct link between the person's outlook on life and their stress hormone levels. An optimist's levels are steady, while a pessimist's soars out of control and become unmanageable.

Optimist versus Pessimist

First, let's take a look at what it means to be an optimist. An optimist is someone who basically believes everything's going to be okay. They don't have a doom and gloom outlook on life, even when something goes wrong. That doesn't mean they ignore times of distress either. But instead of throwing their hands up in the air and giving up (and giving in) to an awful situation, they roll up their sleeves and get to work to make things better.

A pessimist, on the other hand, can't see any positive outcome resulting from a stressful situation at all. They usually imagine the worst case scenario; and even when they don't, they still imagine a situation where nothing good can come of it. Pessimists usually can't understand it, but their outlook is what brings all of that negativity to fruition for them. For example, they go to work "*knowing*" that they'll never get a promotion at work. Their lacklustre attitude affects their work output. The boss doesn't see a go-getter, he sees a miserable employee, so when the time comes for promotions he will choose someone else because he wants a leader—someone who can inspire others. If an optimist gets passed over for the job, they adopt a mindset that has them analysing what went wrong so that they can repair it and get ahead in the near future.

Pessimists Can't Control Their Cortisol

It's not that they don't want to, but a pessimist can't manage his cortisol (the stress hormone) levels once they're disrupted. Not only does the hormone present at a much higher level, but once it's released, the pessimist can't claw their way out of it. What happens to the pessimist when his or her stress levels get out of control on a consistent basis?

➤ *Their Hearts Suffer*

A pessimist suffers from heart disease more than an optimist does. The *Psychological Bulletin* published a scientific review about a study where researchers discovered that optimism actually *protects* you from heart disease to some degree.

➤ *Their Cholesterol Is Out of Control*

The Harvard School of Public Health found in their scientific study that optimists have a better HDL score–

that's the good cholesterol your body needs for optimal health. Pessimists, on the other hand, have to work harder to get their levels up.

> ### They Can't See a Silver Lining During Stressful Situations

The so-called silver lining can help you manage your stress levels. Pessimists see no such lining, but optimists do. Optimists learn from bad events and prevent them in the future.

> ### They Get Sick a Lot

A pessimist has his or her immune system knocked out of whack. An optimist usually has a strong, formidable immune system. Researchers have discovered that an optimist's immune cells cluster and fight off infection better than a pessimist's does.

> ### They Are More Emotionally Unstable

Pessimists can't handle the stress they experience, so they're continually upset and depressed about their circumstances. This is especially prevalent after traumatic events– they just can't recover. But even small stressful situations don't leave them as quickly as would be expected.

➤ *They Die Sooner*

Poor pessimists. Not only is their whole life filled with one disappointment after another, but in the end, they don't survive as long as their positive-minded peers. That's probably because the horrible effects stress has on their health are usually avoided by the optimistic individuals.

Is It Possible to Convert Yourself into an Optimist?

Some people mistakenly believe that optimists are born that way. But this isn't true. You choose how you look at life's ups and downs, and sometimes you have to learn new ways of handling difficult situations if you're not equipped to do that yet. This isn't going to happen overnight. If you've labelled yourself a pessimist– or if others are constantly telling you that you're negative, then you need a complete attitude readjustment because it's time to turn over a new leaf.

What happens whenever you go through a horrible situation? We're not talking about rush hour traffic, but something life-changing, like a round of pink slips in the workplace? Instead of slumping down into a stressed out, anxious state of mind, work to fortify your position at the company. Be realistic and know that your job might not last forever and even before that time comes, have a back-up plan. You can, for instance, improve on your skills and learn new things that make you attractive to employers.

It's time for you to understand that you don't "have bad luck" like many pessimists believe. You have control of your life and the outcome. Some things you can't control— like being late to work because of a traffic jam. But you *can* control the fact that you can plan to leave a bit early each day to give yourself a cushion of time to work with.

If you're currently a pessimist, try surrounding yourself with positive people. Don't bring them down with you— let their mindsets have an influence on you to lift you up to a better place.

It's not just about the people you allow to have an effect on you, it's about everything. From news, movies and shows you watch to the music you listen to— even books you read —t ry to keep it upbeat, or at least keep the negative stuff to a minimum.

If you realise that certain things put you in a better mood, do more of it! It might be a certain scent filling the air in a room with a super sweet aroma, or a specific CD or videos that sets the tone for a better you. I often listen to Christian worship songs to boost my mood.

Change your mindset whenever you catch yourself getting down in the dumps. You might have to keep a record of it at first, recording your moods throughout the day and seeing what triggers a pessimistic response in you.

But over time, you'll also see a pattern of positive triggers. For example, watching the news after work sets you off, but playing a game with your kids lifts your mood. You can spend more time playing and less time informing yourself of what's wrong in the world. Some pessimists make fun of the optimists by saying they're not being realistic. Well neither are you, if you want the honest truth. Instead of being in your head imagining everything that is wrong and how bad it is, seek out conversations with real people who have a better outlook on life.

Train yourself to be a glass-half-full type of person. Whenever you encounter a negative situation that stresses you out, stop, take a deep breath, and consider how it can turn into a positive or at least how it's not as bad as you think it is. If you start to see a real change in your attitude, pat yourself on the back for your efforts. It's not easy making the switch and most people (pessimists especially), never make the effort. The fact that you even attempted it means you're not nearly as pessimistic as you might think you are, because you believe in the possibility that you can change and you will.

In one interesting study, researchers told participants to complete a sentence. One group had to complete a sentence that said, *"I wish I were a …"* and the other had to complete a sentence that said, *"I'm glad I'm not a ..."*

In the first one, the participant had to basically adopt a negative outlook by not being happy with what they currently are. In the second one, they were thankful for what they are and acknowledging that things could have been worse.

Waging War on Pessimism

Right now, as a pessimist, you're putting yourself in a precarious situation. You're risking your health and happiness and possibly having a negative impact (aroma) on those around you. You don't want that! It's time to take matters into your own hands and start managing your stress better. You can do this by working on your positive outlook each day.

Use positive affirmations as a good starting point. These are positive phrases and sentences that get ingrained in your head. Here is a list of positive affirmations that you can post in your house where you'll see them:

a) I believe in myself

b) I am capable of handling difficult situations

c) Life is full of endless opportunities

Choose your daily statement of faith. Meditate on it! Speak it every morning.

➤ Moses would say, **"Lord, if You don't go with us or before us, we are not going anywhere."**

➤ Abraham would say, **"The Lord will provide."**

➤ Jacob would say, **"I won't let go of You unless You bless me."**

➤ Joshua would say, **"As for me and my house, we will serve the Lord."**

➤ Samuel would say, **"Speak, Lord, for your servant is listening."**

➤ Nehemiah would say, **"The joy of the Lord is my strength."**

➤ David would say, **"The Lord is my Shepherd, I shall not want,"** and **"This is the day that the Lord has made and I will rejoice and be glad in it."**

➤ Solomon would say, **"Trust in the Lord, oh my soul, and lean not on your own understanding, in all your ways acknowledge Him and He shall direct your path."**

➤ Isaiah would say, **"Arise and shine for my Glory has come."** and **"No weapon formed against me shall prosper."**

➤ Jeremiah would say, **"The Lord has plans to prosper me and not to harm or fail me."**

➤ Jabez would say, **"Oh, that you may bless me and enlarge my territory."**

➤ Shadrach, Meshach and Abednego would say, **"We will not bow down to any image but will serve the Lord."**

➢ Ezekiel would say, **"Any dry bones in my life, live again."**

Now it's your turn… *what would you say?*

When I started writing this book, I had to keep reminding myself of my unique price tag, believing I had all it takes to keep pressing on to the last page, it took me a while, but I was never going to change my price tag.

Whatever your plans are, please get to work now because I believe you are going to make it. You have the aroma factor to accomplish it. *YES, YOU CAN.*

Chapter Nine

GOD WILL NEVER CHANGE HIS PRICE TAG

His aroma is still the same yesterday, today and forever. There is no price tag involved when it comes to God and His Word. There is nothing new that would take Him by surprise. He said in Malachi 3:6 that *"I am the LORD, I change not."* And because His price tag does not change, ours too remain the same.

Life Empowering Activities that Strengthen Your Self Esteem

It's sometimes difficult to work on your self-esteem and empower yourself to be successful. Television commercials and other social media platforms such as Facebook, Twitter and Instagram aren't always encouraging or positive. In fact, they can be downright discouraging, making you question who you are and what you want to do with your life.

You need to gain power over the negatives in your life by motivating yourself in several ways, including getting off the couch to become healthy and fit. Make the most of your ambitions. You also want to discover how to develop relationships that help rather than sabotage your life, get the education you need to boost your self-esteem and put boundaries in place for those who zap your strength and damage your self-confidence.

Life-empowering activities are good for any age group. They can bring fun and learning into an otherwise boring and staid existence and even add years to your life. When you train your mind to think with self-esteem building thoughts, you'll also be learning new skills for building relationships, business success and personal success.

Getting Healthier and Fit

You don't have to be a rocket scientist to know that if you're sitting in front of a computer screen during the day and on the couch at night, you're not doing much to boost your health and fitness quotient.

Self-confidence and health are sure to wane when you live a sedentary lifestyle because those endorphins– so important to your mind – aren't being produced. Feeling strong and enjoying a high energy level are imperative to your attitude, outlook on life and self-esteem every day. Get into a routine of exercise you enjoy, one that gives you a good combination of cardio and strength building. Your heart, bones and mind will benefit and you'll lower your risk of high blood pressure, weight gain and chances of anxiety and depression.

Simply planning a good exercise program that fits your needs, wants and likes can be an incredible boost to your self-esteem. But it will only work if you stick to it, so mix it up and keep it fun and exciting. That may mean joining a class or enlisting a friend to exercise with you. Consider anything that will set up the workout time as moments you look forward to rather than dread because of boredom or lack of interest and self-motivation.

You'll also want to set a time for exercise that will fit into your schedule. If you have to get up 30 minutes to an hour earlier to fit in your workout, do it. Eventually, your body and mind will adjust to the new routine and you'll even look forward to it.

The boost of self-esteem that you'll realise with regular exercise might astound you. The positive way your body and mind reacts to a good exercise program can only increase your self-confidence and the level of health and fitness you'll enjoy.

Exercise also greatly affects your hormonal levels. Cortisol is a bad hormone if it's flooding your body constantly and it's released when you experience stress and anxiety, so it can affect your moods, well-being and feelings of self-esteem.

Beta-endorphins are the enemies of the cortisol hormone. You don't have to experience high intensity aerobic exercise to enjoy the benefits that come with releasing beta-endorphins into your system.

A few minutes of moderate aerobic exercise will do the job nicely. Don't forget meditation in your daily exercise routine. Deep breaths and stretches can help lessen tension levels and reduce anger and depression. You'll enjoy elevated mental acuity. Your diet plan is also important in your quest to become healthy.

It's important to pay attention to your cravings and to plan a diet around healthy foods that combat weight gain and health risks such as heart disease, high blood pressure and diabetes.

Setting health and fitness goals and reaching them, step-by-step, will provide the inner strength you'll need to reach other goals in your life. Your self-esteem will soar because of the inner belief you gain that you can really do it.

Giving Yourself a Success Makeover

You've heard of and have probably experienced a makeover in terms of hair, makeup and other physical beauty enhancements. It's great to treat yourself once in a while because it helps your self-confidence. But, you can also give yourself a success makeover to boost your self-esteem and make you ready for whatever life throws at you. It is possible to plan a makeover for whatever is holding you back and zapping your self-esteem in any area of your choice. Want to make more money, improve your health, get rid of your fears or find your true calling? Prepare for a success makeover.

As humans, we're born motivated to succeed. We're motivated to eat, crawl, walk, learn lessons in school and take the actions needed to enjoy the fruits of our labour. But sometimes something happens along the way to discourage us and make us quit trying.

Excuses and blaming others for our failures only promote pessimism and low self-esteem. We occasionally see ourselves as victim and quit trying or delay our success because of pre-conceived notions that we are just not good enough. The vision (aroma) dies and we are left with a life not lived to the fullest. Giving yourself a success makeover can lift you out of the ashes of failed past attempts and breathe new life into your goals and dreams to regenerate your aroma.

It all begins when you start to energise your life by revamping your vision of the future and being a little tougher on yourself. You may have some goals you want to ultimately reach, but it is possible you feel lost or got distracted along the way. It's easy to get off track because of all the stresses of the world; and to get back on track, you have to work just as hard as you did in the beginning. You may need to upgrade to a new set of rules based on your passions and interests of today rather than yesterday.

First, ask yourself if the path you're on right now will lead you to your ultimate life goals. If your wish and plan is to be fit and healthy and you never exercise and give in to your sugar and carb cravings, you'll likely never reach that goal. If you wish to write a book and you never put pen to paper, it just remains a wish; you will never become an author. It's the same with business or personal successes. Are you doing what you need to do to reach goals you've set for yourself? Do you daydream about future success or simply count the hours and minutes until the end of the day?

If you answered yes, you're likely disconnected from your job or whatever it is you're working on. Rethink your career or commitments and don't be afraid to change in mid-stream. Your aroma has no age limit.

If you're going to be bored or unchallenged, it's not worth another minute of your cherished time. But when you do make a firm commitment, stick with it and see it to the end.

Another way to achieve a success makeover is to educate yourself. Only then will you gain the knowledge, develop the skills and promote credibility enough to achieve ultimate success in the field you've chosen.

Cherish your time and don't put off things until the last minute. That will only cause stress and increase the chance that you won't complete the tasks at hand. Day planners, reminders on your phone and ticking off tasks on a list are all good ways to be organised and keep you motivated to carry out the next set of tasks. Pay attention to your finances. Understanding your expenses and learning how to manage your money properly will prevent finding yourself in a quagmire of bills and an overspending cycle that's difficult to get out of.

Take time to enjoy the moment. Don't dwell on your past failures, but use them as a stepping stone to future successes. Live life in the here and now rather than in the past and don't waste time daydreaming about the future.

A success makeover should include some life-empowering activities that will strengthen your self-esteem and make it possible to achieve all your goals and dreams. Inactivity will ensure you never reach them. *Rise up and activate your aroma now.*

Developing Relationships

Develop relationships that encourage, rather than discourage you - and make sure they help you continue on the path you've chosen. Whether the relationship you're developing is business oriented or personal, your self-esteem and ability to achieve your goals and dreams can be affected. Relationships take work, and you can develop more positive relationships in your life by following a few simple rules of engagement such as listening effectively. Make eye contact and strive to listen carefully to those you're interacting with. Empathise with people. You may not have walked in their shoes, but you can empathise with what they're going through by developing an understanding. Learn and develop communication skills that will help you better understand and draw out the best in others. We're all so different in so many ways. Learn to celebrate those differences rather than constantly striving to get others to come around to your way of thinking and doing things.

Your time is valuable. Giving it to another person is an incredible gift and should be given wisely, but fully. When you choose to be with another person, be devoted to them in terms of the energy you give and how effectively you communicate. This will serve to build rather than erode that relationship.

Technology Can Bring New Challenges

A new caveat on the relationship scene is how you manage your mobile devices. Almost everyone has a cell phone – they're a wonderful tool for communication, especially in emergency situations. But these devices can also distract you from listening attentively to the person you're with and keep you from being completely in the moment. Learn how to manage them by turning them off or using the settings feature to only accept calls from people you need to monitor– such as children. It is so annoying when discussing business or any other important matter dear to you and the other person is constantly checking messages and replying comments on social media; it gives the wrong signal. Do not waste your time with such people, they are obviously not listening, it is very rude, no wonder such people are less productive.

Trust

Trust is a huge part of any relationship as is respect. It takes a lot of self-confidence to trust another person, but it's imperative if you want to support and become part of another person's life.

Opening your heart and mind to another person is an act of trust that can boost your self-esteem and strengthen ties in a relationship. Make sure that the relationship you want to pursue is positive. Don't engage in a relationship where you feel inferior or one that's otherwise damaging to your self-confidence. Every now and then, it might be worth giving it some time to build trust. Time reveals all things. The temptation to go all out when we meet people in the first few days is very high but from experience, I realised that we all put on our best to impress our new friends or people we meet. Aroma cannot be camouflaged, just give it a bit of time and listen more.

Most people have rushed into friendships, marriages and even business relationships just too soon and later find out that it was just a borrowed and false aroma.

Tread cautiously and be intentional with your words and the extent to which you share information. Do not swallow everything you hear too quickly, learn to chew on it a bit. I tell you, you will save yourself a lot of headache and thank the aroma factor for it. Love at first sight has destroyed many. Don't open up too quickly until you get to identify the true aroma of the other person.

Educating Yourself

Nothing is a better self-esteem booster than education. Education arms you with facts and know-how to act on your goals and accomplish what you want to do in life. And it's the best type of investment you can make to your future success. That doesn't necessarily mean you have to get a bachelor's, master's or doctorate degree, but other types of education such as reading books, online studies, finding a mentor in your chosen profession, and attending conferences and seminars are all types of education which can propel you to attaining your chosen life goals. Your brain is a muscle— and like the muscles in your arms and legs, it needs stimulation, too. If you don't use your brain, it will deteriorate just as your other muscles do when you don't use them enough. In our world today, information changes so rapidly that it's tough to keep up with it —especially in computer science. Continuing education is imperative if you want to continue a career in computers, otherwise your knowledge will become completely obsolete in a couple of years.

Self-esteem is also learned. The empowering activities you're learning now will help you master any challenge that comes your way. Each activity requires practice– the only way to reach the end result of high self-esteem. Learning new things and having new experiences can keep your body as well as your mind youthful.

Putting Boundaries in Place

Setting boundaries within your personal and business areas to boost your self-esteem is necessary to keep your goals and dreams in the forefront of your mind.

Boundaries are an essential part of building healthy relationships that lead to a healthy and happy life.

When you understand your limits and the triggers and actions that breach those boundaries, you'll begin to understand just what makes you tick. First, you have to identify your emotional, mental, spiritual and physical limits. Know what makes you uncomfortable or stresses you out.

When you have that straight in your mind, you'll be better able to recognise the breaches and put up boundaries that get rid of that discomfort and lowers the stress factor.

Guilt and resentment start to creep in to your aroma when your boundaries are crossed. Those are good feelings to recognise. They help you realise when someone has overstepped those boundaries.

You may need to have a conversation with someone who constantly oversteps his boundaries and makes you uncomfortable or damages your self-esteem. A good conversation can become an empowering activity that ensures you'll strengthen your self-esteem by making others aware of who you really are and what you believe.

Awkwardness may occur if you're new to setting boundaries, but eventually, you'll get the hang of it and feel good about maintaining your sense of self. Much of how you react to those who overstep the boundaries you set has to do with how you were raised. For example, if you were a family member's caregiver, you likely focused all of your attention on someone else. You may still be focusing on others too much and ignoring your own physical and emotional needs.

Self-awareness is a mental activity you can practice to become acutely aware of your feelings and then figure out how you're going to deal with broken boundaries. Taking control of a situation that makes you uncomfortable can boost your self-esteem and make you more confident about the boundaries you're setting.

Never let fear or guilt cloud your boundaries. You don't have to simply cope with a situation that makes you feel uncomfortable or like you're being taken advantage of. Speak up for yourself and let others know you've set certain boundaries and they have to honour them for you if they want to be a part of your life.

It is not enough to hide under religion as we've been made to believe, that as a Christian, you need to forgive and forget even when it hurts and your boundaries clearly have been broken. We need to learn to teach people how to treat us.

Healthy relationships are built on boundaries and self-respect. Give yourself permission to set boundaries and do the tasks necessary to make your world all that you need and want it to be.

Life-empowering activities are vital to your self-esteem and to your future success. They can provide you with the mindset you need to accomplish everything you want and to stay focused on what truly matters.

This isn't something that will just materialise when you become aware of it. It's something you have to create a plan for and implement as action steps so that you start to see real change in how you approach your dreams and goals.

Chapter Ten

YOU ARE THE AROMA OF GOD

Your sense of smell has the greatest potential to awaken a variety of emotions within you. The Bible uses the experience of smell to create certain images and teach certain lessons.

In Genesis 8:21, after the great flood had cleansed the earth of sin Noah offered a sacrifice of thanksgiving to God. The Lord smelled the soothing aroma, denoting that the violence and sin were replaced by peace and righteousness. We are to God the pleasing aroma of Christ. Which of the five senses bring back your memories most sharply? For me it is definitely the sense of smell. A certain kind of sun oil takes me instantly to a

French beach. The smell of fish pie brings back the memories of childhood visits to my grandmother. A hint of pine says "Christmas," and a certain kind of aftershave reminds me of my nephew's teenage years.

Paul reminded the Corinthians that they were the aroma of Christ: "For we are to God the pleasing aroma of Christ" (2 Cor. 2:15).

As believers, we are victorious soldiers. And when the gospel of Christ is preached, it is a pleasing fragrance to God.

When we walk with God, people will notice, because we are made of the sweet aroma of God.

As the aroma of Christ, what perfumes do you bring with you as you walk into a room? It's not something that can be bought in a bottle or a jar. When we spend a lot of time with someone, we begin to think and act like that person. Spending time with Jesus will help us spread a pleasing fragrance to those around us.

Lord, please shape my thoughts and actions so people may sense that I have been with You.

Insight

The imagery of a pleasing aroma coming up before the Lord appears in several different ways in Scripture. In Revelation 8:3–4, incense is offered on the altar in heaven. This incense is connected to the prayers of the people of God. *"We see that not only can our lives be a pleasing aroma to God, but our prayers can be as well."* —Bill Crowder

The Importance of Keeping Up with Prayer

Prayer provides people with the opportunity to share all aspects in life with the Heavenly Father. Life's circumstances always change on a daily basis, and the future is yet to unfold. As a matter of fact, things can always go from good to worse in just a very short period of time. God wants people to bring their problems and concerns to Him, and He wants them to become closer to Him all the time. With every blessing that you receive in this life, prayer provides you with an opportunity to express your gratitude for all the things in this life that He gives. Of course, you must constantly give thanks to God for everything He provides. You pray to acknowledge all the blessings and abundance that you have because of Him. All people commit mistakes each day, and they all sin every day, whether they are aware of it or not. You are not perfect but God wants you to recognise your sins and repent, and you can only achieve this through connecting with God. Is your life a sweet aroma to the father?

It is my prayer that you will never lose the identity given to you by God. A good person leaves an inheritance for their children's children, but a sinner's wealth is stored up for the righteous. (Proverb 13:22)

A good man brings good things out of the good stored up in his heart, and an evil man brings evil things out of the evil stored up in his heart. For the mouth speaks what the heart is full of. (Luke 6:45)

This is worth repeating, always remember you are salt and light of the world.

"You are the salt of the earth. But if the salt loses its saltiness, how can it be made salty again? It is no longer good for anything, except to be thrown out

and trampled underfoot. You are the light of the world. A town built on a hill cannot be hidden. Neither do people light a lamp and put it under a bowl. Instead they put it on its stand, and it gives light to everyone in the house. In the same way, let your light shine before others, that they may see your good deeds and glorify your Father in heaven."—Matthew 5:13-16.

Keep shining; never allow anything to take away your sparkle. YOU are precious and unique. Exhibit the god nature in you to deodorise your world. When you do, it will build character in you. This I termed the GUTS of Aroma.

> G-*grateful*
>
> U- *Unoffendable*
>
> T- *Teachable*
>
> S-*Surrendered*

Become a positive expression of God's Aroma.

Chapter Eleven

YOUR AROMA AFTER DEATH

The reality is that when you die, everyone is going to say something about you—people you knew and those you didn't.. Whether they attend your funeral or not, they are all going to make a few comments about how you have impacted their lives. My question to you is: what would they say about you? Who would speak for you? Your aroma will speak for you. Your aroma will be your spokesperson. Be sure you have given it a story worth telling while you still have the chance to do so.

A few months ago, the Wizard of Westwood, John Wooden died after a storied life of triumph. He was arguably one of the greatest coaches and leaders of all time, indelibly influencing the game of basketball forever with his focus on basic skills, team greatness, and individual commitment. I was amazed by how many people he influenced during his life, even long after he stopped coaching. You could tell that his aroma had impacted a lot of people. This inspires me to do more; I also have some work to do on being more authentic with who I am and who I want to become. What do you want your life to be about? If you don't know, it might be the time for you to think about it and start moving towards it today.

The Aroma of Dr. Myles Munroe

Dr. Myles Munroe and his lovely wife, Ruth, have passed on yet the world hasn't stopped talking about them. His publishers have not stopped printing his books because his books are selling more than ever. And like he said in one of his interviews, "You gotta die empty." Myles's aroma is still alive. His aroma lingers on.

The Aroma of Maya Angelou

Maya Angelou is a name that will be very hard to forget even in the next thousand years. Today, Maya Angelou is remembered for her insurmountable contributions to literature, the performing arts and the civil rights movement, and for her indomitable spirit. For her bravery with her personal narrative, many of us have learned not only to celebrate our diversity, but to also honour reality by boldly sharing our personal stories. Even though Maya is dead, she is still alive. That means that we should not *die when we die*. Our names shouldn't fade away immediately we stop breathing; it should continue to breathe. What sort of aroma are you creating?

Chapter Twelve

BLENDING IT ALTOGETHER

I don't know what your personal aroma is. In other words, I don't know what you were put on this earth to do. What I know for sure is, we all have something to do on this earth; a purpose to fulfill. There's a story behind every successful candidate, with ups and downs, trials and tribulations, struggles, disappointments and sacrifices. The reason why successful people have a story to tell is because of the number of failures they've experienced over the years to get there. Without failure, success wouldn't be as sweet. If success was just handed down to you on a silver platter, what would be your inspiring story to encourage others? Failure is inevitable on the quest to greatness.

The potential inside you may not have been realised by others. You might have accepted the opinion of society by the labels they placed on you. Never change your price tag. The truth is there is a treasure box hidden within you so full of untapped spices that you can't even fathom. You still have a wealth of spices inside you now just as you did as a new-born baby. Go in there to blend them up.

We all have a part to play to make the world a better place. It's not a matter of name, position, power or wealth that give you the edge to do great things; it's the passion to do small things in a great way.

In the pursuit of greatness, your spirit won't rest completely until the day your passion is fully revealed. That in turn becomes your motivation for waking up each morning. Along the way, there will be steep mountains to climb, opposition to fight, and your own fears and doubts to overcome. But inside you lie a yielding hope, faith and courage to press on to the end. There is a price to pay for greatness. It doesn't come easily, but your aroma will chauffeur you to your destination. What price are you willing to pay for greatness? What aroma are you stamping on the brains of history?

Today, I encourage you to stay focused. Go within you to manifest your truest self. You have all the spices within you; blend it well to become the happier you!

Go hard or go home…

YOU ARE THE *TRUE EXPRESSION* OF THE *AROMA FACTOR*

Vida Lartey Consultancy Services

Life Strategist | Speaker | Author| Family & Behaviour Therapist

Transforming Your Vision into Reality

Sometimes in life we all need a friend to lean on. We are here for you.

Services:

✧ Strategies for a successful living
✧ Mentorship for Parents and Young People
✧ Life and Workplace Stress Management
✧ Leadership and Self-development Training

We listen ~ We act ~ We deliver

Contact us for a friendly chat:
Mob: 07429925898
E-Mail:
vidartey@yahoo.co.uk
vida@vidalartey.com
Website: www.vidalartey.com

Facebook: *Vida Lartey*
Instagram: *@vidamlartey*
Twitter: *@vidalartey*

NOTES

Books

- There is Nothing New Under the Sun By Warren E. Berkley From Expository Files 19.8; August
- Understanding your Potential by Myles Munroe
- Grit: *The Power of Passion and Perseverance*, May 5, 2016 by Angela Duckworth
- Young Entrepreneur Council, By Andrew Vest
- Claire Dorotik-Nana
- *Websites*
- http://www.biblestudy.org/question/how-long-did-it-take-noah-to-build-ark.html
- http://www.nexera.com
- The Story of Maya Angelou https://relevantmagazine.com/culture/books/legacy-maya-angelou
- https://www.uhs.umich.edu/tenthings
- J.K Rowling story inspired: http://www.thisisinsider.com/jk-rowling-facts-harry-potter-author-life-2017-7#the-harry-potter-novels-werent-always-released-around-the-world-at-the-same-time-11
- Lance Armstrong story inspired by: https://www.vanityfair.com/news/2008/09/armstrong2008
- http://www.beliefnet.com/faiths/christianity/5-greatest-friendships-of-the-bible.aspx?p=5#uufwxYeXCu2VusDF.99
- 2012http://www.bible.ca/ef/expository-ecclesiastes-1-4-11.htm
- http://www.eattasteheal.com/eth_6tastes.htm
- http://www.icr.org/earths-water

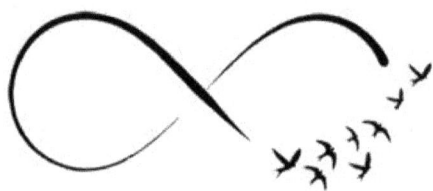

YOUR AROMA
IS LIMITLESS

www.ingramcontent.com/pod-product-compliance
Lightning Source LLC
LaVergne TN
LVHW051557080426
835510LV00020B/3019